How To Fix Your Own Clock

By Richard Hansen

Goofy Rooster Publishing
Wylie, Texas
www.goofyrooster-publishing.com

How To Fix Your Own Clock

By Richard Hansen

Goofy Rooster Publishing   PO Box 2904 Wylie, Texas 75098
www.goofyrooster-publishing.com

ISBN-10: 0-9843940-9-5

ISBN-13: 978-0-9843940-9-8

Photo credits: front cover photo by Peter Manik Copyright ©2011 (model: Julie Christine). Photo of author on back cover by Peter Manik.

For My Father, Robert I. Hansen,

who had me convinced when I was a child,

that he could do anything...

The Questions

Introduction

I've written this book as a series of questions and answers. They are all taken from my past newspaper columns, and are intended to give clock owners (whether they own pendulum or windup clocks) some basic knowledge on how to get their clocks running and keep them running (without the need to take them to the repair shop).

I hope you find the information useful.

Richard Hansen

The Answers

1. What Are The Basic Parts Of A Clock?

Hands

Those things that you look at to see what time it is. The short one is the hour hand, and the longer one is the minute hand. Some clocks also have a second hand, which moves fast, one turn around in a minute.

Pendulum

If your clock has something that swings back and forth, that is the pendulum. On a 400 day anniversary clock, the four little balls that spin back and forth act as a pendulum.

Weights

Some clocks (mostly grandfather clocks) have brass colored round objects (about 2 inches in diameter, and 6 inches or so long) which hang on chains, pulleys, or thin cords. On cuckoo clocks, those things that look like pine cones are the weights.

Power Source

A clock is a machine, so it needs power to run (like a car needs gasoline). Clocks normally get this power from a long coiled spring, a weight, a battery or electricity from a wall outlet.

Gear Train

A series of shafts and gears that use the power source to drive a time indicator. Even quartz clocks have a gear train if they have hands! The only clocks or watches that do not have gears are those with a digital time indicator.

Time Indicator

The hands in front of a dial, a bell, or chimes that are sounded at regular intervals. The first clocks (fifteenth century) had no hands - only a bell to sound the passing hours.

Escapement

Something to control the power source and let the power "escape" at only a fixed rate, similar to the gas pedal or cruise control on a car. Escapements include the watch balance wheel, the quartz crystal, the "floating balance" (invented in the 50's), and the well-known pendulum.

If a clock runs too fast or too slow, it's usually the fault of the escapement. Almost all escapements can be adjusted for rate (speed). For a pendulum clock, this adjustment is usually assumed by a clock man to be the responsibility of the clock owner.

Chime

If a clock plays some part of a melody every 15 minutes - it is *chiming* (NOT *striking*).

Strike

Most clocks *strike* the hour count on each hour (they do NOT *chime* the hour).

Bob

The disk at the bottom end of the pendulum.

2. How Do I Set Up A Shelf Clock?

If you are not going to run your shelf clock, it can be located anywhere that you would want to display a nice decorative item. If you do wish to run it, then it should be located on a reasonably solid surface that doesn't move or vibrate with normal traffic in the room. The surface should be approximately level.

Setting Up And Starting The Clock

Hang the pendulum on the clock, then wind the clock. Position the clock where you want it to reside. Check it for rocking - see that it is stable. If necessary, put spacers (coins, cardboard, etc.) under one or two corners or feet to prevent rocking.

If you can easily reach the pendulum, just give it a light push to start it swinging in an arc wide enough to make the clock tick. Or (with the clock in place), raise one end of the clock about 1 or 2 inches, then pause and put it down. This should swing the pendulum enough to start it. If it doesn't, try again.

Putting The Clock "In Beat" (see question #5)

This applies only to pendulum driven clocks. Making a clock level, and putting a clock "in beat" are not necessarily the same thing. Given a choice: **a clock does not have to be level to run - but it must be "in beat."**

A correctly adjusted clock runs best on a level surface. However, clocks can be knocked out of adjustment by moving them around and, in most cases, they cannot be easily readjusted.

If out of adjustment, you will need to prop up one end of the clock. As a start, set the clock so that it LOOKS level - don't use a carpenter's level, spirit level or any other kind of device for determining this.

To put the clock "in beat" is not difficult. A clock is "in beat" if the time from tick to tock is equal to the time from tock to tick. This sounds silly, but it is easy to understand if - when you have the clock running - you raise one end of the clock slightly and listen to the sound. Put that end down, then raise the other end. You will hear a change in the "beat." Do this several times to train your ear.

Once you can tell by sound what is "in beat" for your clock, you may have to prop up one end of it to keep that sound. Use coins, paper, or whatever is necessary to raise one end of the clock to make it run with the best beat. Listen to the clock over a few minutes to be certain that as it settles down in its running; it is still in good beat.

3. How Do I Hang A Wall Clock (Including Cuckoo Clocks)?

Where To Hang Your Wall Clock

Wall clocks should be hung on a wall where they will be out of the way of heavy traffic - where people won't accidently bump it (e.g.: not next to the front door). It can be on an inside or outside wall. Cuckoo clocks, however, should NOT be hung in a drafty area. Cuckoo clock pendulums are light in weight, and are not "streamlined" - they're not made to slip through the air with little resistance. Most other clocks have stream-lined pendulum bobs - flat smooth disks (and that design is not for looks). The breeze through an open window can be enough to stop a cuckoo clock.

What To Hang It On

If the clock is weight driven, or is at all heavy - it should be hung on a nail driven into a wall stud, or on a molly bolt. The "head" of the item you hang it on should be small enough to fit in the hole on the back of the clock, but large enough so that the clock definitely won't pull away and fall.

Hang the clock on the nail (or molly bolt), then hang the pen-dulum on the clock. Hang the weight(s), if any, on their re-spective pulleys/hooks. Be sure the cords are correctly in the grooves of the pulley wheels. On weight driven clocks, be sure that the cords up in the clock are over the drums on which the cords are wound - NOT tucked down between the drum and the plate of the clockworks.

Leveling The Clock - Left To Right

Do NOT use a spirit level or a carpenter's level. Move the bottom of the clock to the right or left until the clock LOOKS level to you. If the clock has a centering scale or centering marker of some sort on the inside, then you can use that. Position the clock so that the motionless pendulum is aligned with the marker center.

Putting The Clock Flush Against The Wall

Look to see that the top and bottom of the clock's back are both against the wall (unless your clock is a Vienna Regulator - more on this in a couple of paragraphs). Check that the clock will not wobble - press either bottom corner of the clock to test. If it does, do something to stop the wobble - put spacers of some sort behind the clock.

If the clock has "levelers" - use them. The "levelers" are found on either bottom corner of some older European clocks (usually on the outside), and look like screws with large gnarled heads for turning by hand. The sharp end of the screw is aimed at the wall and, when turned clockwise, will move toward the wall to stabilize the clock.

Push start the pendulum to get it swinging back and forth. Listen for any rubbing sounds and watch it for erratic bumping or swaying as it goes back and forth. Do not be overly concerned yet as to whether it is ticking correctly. If the pendulum is hitting something, you will probably need to move the top or bottom of the clock away from the wall so that it swings freely. It is quite common to need to do this with Vienna Regulators. They usually need the top of the clock to be ½ to ¾ inches out from the wall to keep the pendulum from rubbing on the inside back of the case.

In some cases, the top of the clock will stay out if you just reposition it on the nail. In other cases, you may need a spacer (pencil, strip of wood, paper, etc). And sometimes it's the bottom of the clock that needs to be away from the wall.

Wind The Clock

Wind it. There is no set direction to wind all clocks. Some wind counter-clockwise, some clockwise. The directions may even be different on different winding arbors that are on the same clock.

Putting The Clock "In Beat"

This is the most important thing of all to do when hanging any wall clock. If you do not put your clock "in beat," it will not run. Putting it "in beat" is different than making it level. For instructions on putting your wall clock "in beat" (including for cuckoo clocks), see question #5.

4. What More Should I Know When Hanging Cuckoo Clocks?

If the chains are tempting to a child or pet, hang the cuckoo clock behind a couch or some other obstruction. The clock should be hung on a nail with a head small enough to fit in the hole on the back of the clock, but large enough so that the clock definitely won't pull away and fall. Cuckoo clocks have relatively light pendulums, and a slight breeze, draft or gust of wind can stop them. Do NOT hang one in a "breezeway."

Once you have the clock on the wall, hang the pendulum on the wire loop that sticks out of the slot on the bottom of the clock (it should be behind the holes through which the chains are hanging). Next, hang the two or three weights on the chain hooks (on a cuckoo clock, it never matters which weight goes on which hook). Check to see if there is a wire through the chains directly under the case (it's there to keep the chains from going back up into the clock while you are transporting it). If you find one there - remove it.

Putting The Clock Flush Against The Wall
(for cuckoo clocks only)

Often, when you put the weights on a cuckoo clock (or as soon as your back is turned), the top of the clock will move out from the wall as far as it can until the nail head catches on the inside of the clock. If this is only a tiny bit - it's not a problem. If it's as much as a ½ inch though, you should drive the nail in further (or do some other trick). The MAIN requirement is for the wire loop the pendulum hangs on to not touch the wood front or back of the slot in the bottom of the clock. If the clock is tipped on the wall in such a way that the wire loop touches the wood, then the clock will not run.

Now see question #5.

5. How Do I Put A Clock "In Beat"?

Note: this section assumes that you have your wall clock hung, the pendulum is on it, the weights are on it (if it's a weight driven clock), and the clock is fully wound.

"Level" Versus "In Beat"

"Level" is when the clock looks level to the eye.

"In Beat" is when the clock runs with an even tick-tock-tick-tock beat, with the same time duration from tick to tock as from tock to tick.

A clock correctly adjusted at the factory (or by your friendly repair person) will be "in beat" when it is level. Nevertheless, this is a very sensitive adjustment - simply taking the clock home, or putting on the pendulum can sometimes change this adjustment.

A level clock will not run if it is very far "out of beat."

Now - Putting The Clock "In Beat"

Give the pendulum a little push to either side and let it go, enough that you can hear the clock start to tick - then listen carefully to it to get the rhythm of the tick-tock-tick-tock. When you have the rhythm sound in mind, move the bottom of the clock a bit to the right (or left) and notice that the rhythm changes. Move the clock back to get the original rhythm, then move it slightly to the other side and notice a change again. Educate your ear to what your clock sounds like "in" and "out" of beat.

Now position the clock so that the rhythm is *most* even... so that the tick-tock-tick-tock sound has the most even

timing between the ticks and the tocks.

Let the clock settle down for a minute or two, then listen again. Readjust the left-right position as necessary to get the most even beat.

When you are satisfied, mark the position of the clock some-how. Some people make a small pencil mark on the wall, so they can get it back to "in beat" if it is moved.

When clocks taken home from a new purchase (or from a re-pair person) fail to run - the *most common reason* is because they are out of beat (due to being hung/positioned incorrectly by the owner). This reason is more common than all other rea-sons combined!

6. What Makes A Clock Run Too Slow Or Too Fast?

No clock keeps perfect time.

To say, "My clock runs 5 minutes slow" means very little. You must say how long it took to be 5 minutes slow, as in "my clock loses 5 minutes in 12 hours." That is radically different than losing 5 minutes in a month. Some have a fairly consistent error, or "rate," while some are erratic. To mean anything, the error rate has to be expressed with two numbers (how much it varies over what period).

Also important is consistency. A consistent error rate is easy for you to adjust, because it is sensitive to the length of the pendulum. An erratic rate is most likely not fixable, and may have various causes such as: humidity, temperature, drafts in the room, barometric pressure, kids and pets in the room, time of the year, and yes - even phases of the moon.

7. How Accurate Can My Clock Be?

The term for clock accuracy is "rate." A rate of +1 minute per day means a clock has a cumulative error whereby it gains 1 minute a day, or 7 minutes a week. A rate can be gaining or losing.

Here are generally the best rates to expect from different types of clocks (without a great deal of adjusting effort):

- *8 day cuckoo:* 1 minute per week.

- *Tall case clock that has a wooden pendulum rod, and strikes or chimes:* 20 seconds per week.

- *Tall case clock that has a wooden pendulum rod, but does not strike or chime:* 10 seconds per week.

- *Spring driven clocks:* run faster when fully wound than when almost unwound...so, if you wind a well adjusted 8 day pendulum clock on Sunday night, expect it to be somewhat fast by Wednesday and back on time by the next Sunday.

- *Quartz clocks:* vary in accuracy - from super accurate, to a rate of 1 or 2 minutes per month.

- *Clocks with a "Floating Balance" escapement:* can be very accurate for several years, with a rate like just a few seconds per month. After a few years, though, they begin to slow down. When they are almost ready to stop from need for servicing (or winding) they may speed up, gaining as much as 10 to 45 minutes per day.

- *Typical early American 8-day shelf clock:* might get down to 30 seconds a week, BUT they have one-minute of slack in the minute hand gearing. The clock will have one minute of difference between when the hand is rising to the hour, and when the hand is falling past the hour. The weight of the minute hand does it. Think about it.

8. My Clock Has 3 Key Holes To Wind On The Dial (Located Below The Dial's Center) - What Are They For?

The center one winds the spring that powers the time gear train - which makes the hands go around.

The right one winds a spring that powers the chime gear train - so that the clock will chime every 15 minutes.

The left one powers the gear train that makes the clock strike the hour (3 at three o'clock, 4 at four o'clock), etc.

9. Why Is There A Small Hole In The Top Of The Dial With A Square Shaft Sticking Out Of It?

On some clocks - there is a small hole in the top of the dial, with a square ended shaft in the hole, and on the dial there may be an "S" on one side and an "F" on the other, as indicators for how to make the clock go slower or faster.

You turn the small square ended shaft in the hole toward the "S" to make the clock run slower, and toward the "F" to make it run faster. Do not turn it more than 5 or 6 turns or you may damage it.

10. Why Does My Pendulum Clock (Grandfather, Cuckoo Or Shelf Clock) Run Too Fast?

The pendulum is too short. See question #12.

11. Why Does My Pendulum Clock (Grandfther, Cuckoo Or Shelf Clock) Run Too Slow?

The pendulum is too long, See question #12.

12. How Do I Adjust The Pendulum On My Weight Driven Grandfather Clock?

Read All Of This Answer Before Beginning!

You can make the pendulum shorter or longer by moving the bob (the round disk at the lower end of the pendulum) up or down. This changes the weight distribution on the pendulum and makes it effectively feel longer or shorter to the clock.

To move the bob up or down, you turn the nut below it, which in turn drives the bob up or lets it slide down. However plain or fancy the pendulum may be, it will have a large round disk (called the bob) near the bottom end, and below that a nut which can be turned on the threaded shaft which sticks out at the absolute bottom end. The working length of the pendulum is measured from the top where it swings down to the center of the pendulum bob. Moving the bob is what changes the length of the pendulum (and turning the nut is what moves the bob).

If you move the bob UP, you make the pendulum shorter, and the clock runs faster. You move the bob up when you turn the nut to your right, (i.e.: moving the front side of the nut facing you to your right).

The first thing to do is to be sure that your clock indeed runs too fast or too slow. Set it to agree with some known accurate time source, perhaps a TV channel with a time indicator. Then let the clock run until it very definitely disagrees with the time source by several minutes.

Suppose it loses 7 minutes in two days. You will want to make the pendulum "shorter":

Stop the pendulum.

With a marker (felt tip, magic marker, etc.), mark one point on the nut that is on the bottom of the pendulum so that you can keep track of how many turns you turn it.

Turn the nut (the side facing you) to your right until you have turned it a significant amount: at least 4 turns, but not more than 10 turns (if you use smaller adjustments, e.g.: only ¼ of a turn at a time, it may take you six months to get the clock right). For this example, let's say you did 8 turns.

Write down (somewhere) that you adjusted the nut, which way, and how many turns you adjusted it.

Start the clock, and set it to your accurate source.

When you know the clock is definitely wrong again, either too fast or too slow (which may take hours or days) - adjust it again. If it is still running slow, adjust the nut to the right again the same number of turns (in our example, 8). Start it, set it and run it again until it is definitely too fast or too slow. Repeat until the clock is running too fast.

The first time you find that you have overshot and the clock is now running too fast, reverse the adjustment and adjust the nut down (turn it left) by half of what you last turned it up (in this case, you would turn it 4 turns down). Be careful here that when you move the nut down (when you turn it left) that the bob indeed follows it. Some bobs can become stuck on the threaded shaft and do not easily fall when the nut is moved downward. The bob MUST move down.

Set and run the clock again until it is definitely wrong. If it now runs too slow again, adjust the nut up (turn it right) 2 turns. If it still runs too fast, adjust the nut down (turn it left) 2 turns.

Set and run the clock again until it is definitely wrong. Depending on whether it is too fast or too slow - move the nut up (right) or down (left) by 1 turn. You should be very close to having a fairly accurate clock.

By now, you should have an idea of the strategy that I use. Make BIG adjustments until you overshoot, then adjust in the other direction by ½ the adjustment you last made. You should have the clock corrected in just a very few steps. Start with 4 to 10 turns - just a large enough number so that you make a significant difference.

Just to give you an example of how important it is to start with fairly large adjustments: imagine if the clock eventually took 19 turns to get it right, and you were adjusting it by only 1/4 turn each time...it would take you 76 days to get it right if you made one adjustment every day!

13. How Do I Make My Cuckoo Clock Run Faster (Or Slower)?

You adjust the pendulum.

Almost all cuckoo pendulums have two parts, a stick with a metal hook on the top end to hook it to the clock, and another piece of wood on a slider clamp of some sort, which allows you to slide it up and down on the first part (the stick). This second part is usually (but not always) shaped like a leaf. Slide the "leaf" up the stick to make the clock run faster, or down to make the clock run slower.

BEFORE you slide the leaf anywhere, however, decide how to mark the stick so that after you've moved it, you'll know where it was to begin with. If the clock is running slow and you intend to move the leaf UP, you might make a pencil line on the stick just at the bottom of the clip. Then move the leaf/clip up about an inch on the stick, and wind, set, and start the clock.

If the clock is still slow the next day - again mark where the bottom of the clip happens to be, then move the clip up again another inch. Wind, set and start the clock.

Eventually, the clock will start running too fast. Then you make a mark on the stick at the top of the clip, and move the clip down about a half inch. Now you have a clip that has a mark above it on the stick and below it on the stick - so you know that the clip will need to be somewhere between those two marks for the clock to run at the right speed. You just keep marking and moving until the clock is accurate.

And understand - you will *never* get it perfect, but you can get it close.

14. The Hour Strike On My Clock Is Always 2 Hours Behind The Real Time (E.G.: When The Hands Read 4, The Clock Only Strikes Twice). What Is The Problem?

This is very easy to fix.

The next time the clock strikes, push the *hour* hand backward until it agrees with the strike (DO NOT touch/move the *minute* hand while doing this). If it just struck 7 and the hands read 9, push the hour hand back to 7. Now the hands and strike will agree. The clock will be two hours slow, however - so you'll need to advance the minute hand (pausing to let the clock complete its striking at each hour and half hour) until the hands again read the correct time. Now the strike and hands will agree.

Why was it wrong? Someone (despite all denials) stuck their finger in too far and touched the hour hand while they were moving the minute hand, and dragged the hour hand along. The minute hand is on a key shaft and cannot be moved without turning the shaft that it is located upon. The hour hand is on a smooth shaft and can easily be moved around the clock dial without moving the shaft.

15. The Hour Hand Is Loose And Just Flops Down To Point At 6, No Matter What The Actual Time Is - How Do I Fix This?

Again, this is easy to fix at home.

As noted in question #14, the hour hand is on a smooth shaft. The shaft is also tapered to be larger as you move into the dial of the clock. Most likely, the problem is that the clock's hour hand has moved forward.

Put the hour hand where you want it to point, then press the hub of it in toward the clock dial with just a little force. It should become tight enough to stay where it belongs.

This problem is *very* common on cuckoo clocks.

16. Is It A Problem That The Weights On My 24 Hour Cuckoo Clock Get Very Uneven During Their 24 Hours Of Running?

No. As long as the clock functions, do not worry about it.

The left weight on a 2-weight cuckoo clock drops a very tiny amount (about 0.0003 inches) every time the clock ticks - so it drops at a very constant rate.

The right weight drops about ¼ inch for each cuckoo sound that the clock makes. At 1 o'clock, it drops ¼ inch. At 12 o'clock, it drops 3 inches very quickly. Therefore, the cuckoo weight gets behind, then plays catch-up twice a day.

The same thing happens on an eight-day grandfather clock, but the differences in the weight relative positions are not as pronounced and are not noticeable unless you are very observant.

17. How Many Different Kinds Of Clocks Are There?

As many kinds as you can imagine. They come in an infinite variety. There are ways to group them, however. For example, group by where you put them:

Floor Clocks: Also called long case or tall case. Any clock that sits on the floor - which includes grandfather (over 6'), grandmother (4'6" to 6'), and granddaughter (under 4'6") clocks.

Wall Clocks: Any clock that hangs on a wall.

Shelf Clocks: Any clock that sits on anything but the floor - be it mantel, bracket, table, or shelf. A mantel clock on a mantel becomes a shelf clock if you move it to a shelf. Seriously, the terms are generally interchangeable.

Group by what powers them: spring, weight, battery, electric.

Group by the type of escapement: pendulum, balance wheel, quartz crystal.

18. How Do I Set Up A 400 Day "Anniversary Clock"?

The most fragile part of an anniversary clock is the thin wire upon which the pendulum is suspended. The wire can be broken by a sudden downward force on the pendulum, or by twisting (rotating the pendulum too far around).

When you get your clock, the pendulum will be either locked into position, or unhooked and totally off of the wire (in order to take strain off of it).

Locating The Clock

Place it on some fairly level solid object which is out of the way of normal traffic in the house, and which is not easily shaken.

Unlocking The Pendulum

If it is a new clock, there should be manufacturer's directions in the package for unlocking or for hooking up the pendulum. If you have the clock home from being repaired, the repair person should have instructed you on how to unlock or hook up the clock.

Leveling The Clock

You do NOT need a leveling tool! The surface on which the clock rests should be *close* to level, but it need not be *exactly* level. Most anniversary clocks have a guide cup centered under the pendulum. Some of them also have leveling adjusters built into the feet. Note that each foot has a serrated wheel which, when turned, will make that side of the clock go up or down. Adjust the feet until the bottom center of the pendulum is fairly centered in the guide cup. The clock will then be adequately level.

If it does not have adjustable feet, you will have to put shims at two places under the clock base. Coins or bits of cardboard make good shims. Do 2-point shimming, so that the clock will sit on 3 points, like a 3-legged stool.

Setting The Clock Hands

Set the hands to the correct time by moving the MINUTE hand, forward or backward. You may or may not hear a chattering sound as you move the hands. Either case is OK.

Starting The Pendulum

Whenever touching the pendulum, only hold it in place or exert side pressure - NEVER push down on it.

First, stop the pendulum if it is moving, then let go of it. The pendulum should have four sections, each with a ball - pick one of the balls in your mind. Push the pendulum around until the ball you picked has moved ¾ turns of a circle around. Stop and let go of the pendulum. The clock will begin to run.

Replace the glass and wait about a half hour to be certain that the clock is running correctly. If necessary, move the hands again for correct time. You can adjust the hands while the clock is running - it is not necessary to stop it.

Be sure that the dome does not touch the pendulum as the pendulum turns. Most glass domes fit very loosely in the channel and can be moved to the rear to miss the pendulum.

To Make The Clock Go Faster Or Slower

Expect it to be somewhere between difficult and impossible to get the clock accurate within 3 minutes per week. On the top of the pendulum, you will see a thumb wheel with arrows and a + (fast) sign and a - (slow) sign. Turn this wheel RELATIVE

TO the balls on the pendulum to affect the clock's speed.

Take the glass off and stop the pendulum anywhere in its rotation, being careful to not exert any down pressure. Holding the pendulum by one of its balls to keep it from turning, turn the thumb wheel in the direction you wish (in the direction of the + if you wish the clock to go faster, in the direction of the - if you wish the clock to go slower). Move it only about a quarter turn - a little movement here does a lot to the clock. Now restart the pendulum.

Wait at least a week before you make another adjustment. Compare how fast or slow the clock is as a function of how much you turn the wheel. It may take several adjustments.

The clock should run a year from one winding, but it will keep better time if you wind it every 6 months.

NEVER move the clock without holding onto the pendulum to keep it from spinning. Lock or unhook the pendulum if you move the clock any distance.

If you spin the pendulum more than 1 full turn - you *may* damage it...if you spin it more than 2 turns - you will *definitely* damage it.

19. How Long Should My Clock Run After I Wind It?

It depends.

A clock that is called a "30 hour" is usually designed to run for 30 hours, which means you wind it every day and have some leeway in doing it.

An "8 day" clock is designed to run 8 days, which means you should wind it every 7 days (giving you a margin of safety in case you forget one day).

A modern 30-hour cuckoo clock is designed to run barely 24 hours. By "designed," I mean that the chains are 6 feet long, so that you can hang it at 7 feet above the floor. A repair person can add 6 inches to each chain and the clock will run about 26 hours for you. If you put 12-foot chains on your clock - it will run for 48 hours (however, you will have to hang it 13 feet above the floor).

20. Can I Wind My Clock More Often?

It does NOT hurt a clock to wind it as often as you wish.

Whether it is spring driven or weight driven, you can rewind a clock every hour if your wish. In fact, a spring driven clock will actually keep better time if it's wound more often.

A 400 day anniversary clock will definitely be more accurate if you wind it every 6 months, rather than only once a year as per its design.

If you are going to store a spring drive clock, it is best to let it run down before you pack it away.

21. My Old Clock Strikes Half An Hour Off (When The Minute Hand Is Straight Up To 12, It Strikes Once; And When The Minute Hand Points Straight Down To 6, It Strikes The Number Of Hours). How Can I Fix This?

You can fix this!

Most likely, the problem is simply that you have an old clock that cannot correct itself when the strike gets off count. This often happens when the strike spring runs out of power before the time spring. The strike function stops and the time keeps running until the time spring also runs down.

If you're not so lucky - the problem may have occurred because there is something wrong with the striking gears (and a repair shop will have to fix it). You can tell which problem you have, with the following directions.

First, you need to set the hands right! Touching the minute hand only, turn the hands clockwise until the minute hand is pointed a little bit past straight down, and the clock is striking some hour count. While it is striking, move the minute hand forward to straight up, plus a couple of minutes. The clock should finish striking with the minute hand a couple of minutes past the hour.

Test by moving the minute hand through the half hour. It should only strike once on the half hour. Now, move the minute hand to the next hour and see what count the clock gives you. Whatever it is, move the *hour hand* (WITHOUT touching the minute hand) to agree with the strike just counted, as described in question 14.

You now have the hands where the inside of the clock thinks they are, but the clock most likely is reading the wrong time for the world (i.e.: it's set to the wrong time).

So you have 2 choices - you can either stop the clock and wait until it reads the correct time, or you can manually run the minute hand around the clock (letting it strike each hour and half hour) until the correct time is reached.

If you do all this (and the clock is wound and all else is fine) ...but tomorrow comes and the striking is wrong again - then there is something else wrong, and the clock needs a trip to the repair shop.

22. Why Can't I Get My Clock To Keep Almost Perfect Time?

To varying degrees, the following things affect the timekeeping of a pendulum clock: temperature, humidity, barometric pressure, phase of the moon, and time of the year.

A spring powered clock runs faster when the spring is fully wound than when it is nearly unwound.

A weight driven clock (where the weight is on a chain) runs faster when the clock is almost run down.

Good Luck!

23. What Does "Regulator" Printed On My Clock Mean?

Probably nothing. The "regulator" on very old clocks sometimes meant a measure of the clock's accuracy.

On any clock under a hundred years old, it is a gimmick to impress the unaware customer.

24. What Are Some Clock "Do's And Don't's"?

- You DON'T have to stop the pendulum when you wind a clock (in fact, it's best that you *don't* stop the pendulum before winding your clock).

- DON'T touch the weights or the pendulum when winding a clock. Fingerprints on lacquered brass weights eventually eat through the lacquer and tarnish the brass.

- You DON'T have to "help" the weights. If you feel you must "help" the weight as you pull down on the loose end of the chain, then "help" by gripping the chain just above the weight hook and lifting there. It takes an expensive house call to re-thread a loose chain through the movement if you have accidentally unhooked the weight and the suddenly free chain has run up through the movement and fallen to the floor.

- DON'T try to pull the weights down if you have wound the clock such that the weights appear jammed at the top. Let the clock run. The weights will drop as the clock runs. If you succeed in getting a weight to come down a bit by pulling down on it, you have broken something in the clock.

- DO remember the terminology when you ask questions about your clock:

Pendulum: The thing that swings back and forth

Weight: Heavy things, look like pine cones on a cuckoo clock, brass cylinders on a grandfather clock.

Hands: The pointed things on the dial that go around telling the time.

Hour hand: The shorter of the two main hands.

Minute hand: The front hand, longer of the two main hands. Second hand: Only used on some clocks, moves quickly, goes around once per minute.

Strike: A clock STRIKES the hour when it makes sounds, which count out, the hour, example: at 4 o'clock, it strikes 4 times. It does not *chime* the hour.

Chime: A clock is chiming when it periodically plays several notes of a melody, e.g.: playing several notes of Westminster chimes every 15 minutes.

- DON'T think that "Tempus Fugit" on your clock dial means anything. It is Latin for the old adage, "time flies." It is not a brand name or trademark.

- DO remember that any clock that has "31 days" on the dial was made in Asia. Any apparent American brand name on the dial of such clocks is fake and meaningless.

- DON'T EVER spray anything on the works of a clock, not oil, not WD40...not anything! Some clockmakers refuse to work on a clock if they can smell WD40 in it.

If the required oil in the tiny pivot holes dries up, the clock WILL stop. The gear teeth, however, are supposed to run without ANY oil on them. Be aware that oil on the gear teeth will cause the clock to stop just as surely as no oil on the pivot holes.

- DON'T EVER spray Windex, or anything with ammonia in it, on any brass which has crevices or joints, or on the glass front of a clock if the glass is held in brass. Ammonia eats brass when it can linger in wet form in cracks and hidden spots on the brass.

25. Did I Over Wind My Clock?

NEVER - this is an urban legend!

You did NOT over wind the clock.

This question is most relevant to spring driven clocks (clocks where power is supplied from a wound-coiled spring) than to weight driven clocks (clocks that have a weight hanging on a chain or cable).

It may happen to you one day when you wind a clock that it quickly stops and just won't start running again (it will appear to have no power). Here's what may have happened:

On a spring driven clock, you have a long spring (sort of a ribbon of steel) perhaps 3 feet to 10 feet long. When fully wound, the spring becomes a tight coil, wrapped around a center shaft - something like wrapping a long piece of tape around a pencil. The inner end of the spring is attached to the shaft, and the outer end to a gear. Since the spring wants to be straight and uncoiled, it will try to uncoil and thereby turn the gear to motivate the clock.

When the spring is covered with fresh oil - the coils easily slide over each other, and so the spring moves the gear. When the oil is old, however, and has turned to glue (i.e.: when the oil becomes very thick), the spring will not have the strength to slide over itself. So the clock will stop.

When this happens, the clock just needs an oil change.

26. How Often Should I Get My Clock Serviced?

There are two schools of thought on this. One is trumpeted by repairmen who need work - they will claim you should get a clock serviced every two or three years. (This is the expensive route.)

The other school of thought on this (and it's my view) is that you just let a clock run until it no longer functions - then you get it serviced.

27. Can I Move The Hands On My Clock Backwards?

On any clock that only tells time (i.e.: one that does not strike or chime), you can move the hands backward.

On any clock that strikes or chimes, that was made after 1900 - you can *usually* move the hands backward. The test is to try it, but stop if you meet resistance that feels as if you might bend something. You may meet slight resistance at 5 minutes to the hour, or at 5 minutes before half past the hour. Just a minor click is OK.

On a clock that tells time and strikes, but doesn't chime, you can move hands backward between 20 minutes past the hour and the hour, and from 10 minutes before the hour to half past the hour.

On most tall case clocks made after WWII, you can move the hands backwards as you wish.

On most recent vintage clocks, the chime will self correct if you move the hands forward or backward at will (it will self correct in two hours after you move the hands to correct the time).

On almost all cuckoo clocks, you may NOT move the hands backwards, because the minute hand is held on with a nut. Moving the hands backwards will cause the nut to unscrew, and the minute hand will become loose.

28. Must My Tall Case Clock Be Level To Be "In Beat"?

If the clock was made *before* 1965 - then probably yes. This means that you have a good chance the clock will be "in beat" when it's level.

If the clock was made *after* about 1965, it probably has a self leveling mechanism in the movement so that even if the clock case is not level, the inner movement can make itself level or "in beat" - with some help from you:

First, you must make the clock case be close to level, then make sure that it does not rock like a chair with one short leg.

Finally, push the pendulum all the way to one side, and let it fully swing from side to side with a large swing. Let it settle down and the swing will diminish. As it settles down, it will self adjust to make the clock beat settle on a fairly level position. The clock will believe it is level, and so it will run.

About The Author

Richard Hansen is an electrical engineer who graduated from Auburn University. He worked for years in California in the Silicon Valley as a design engineer. After taking night classes in clock repair, the hobby interest in clocks he had developed over the years grew to become a career change.

Richard is a second generation clock person (his father owned 800 clocks at one time). Since changing careers, Richard has taught beginning and advanced clock repair in California, Pennsylvania, New York, and Connecticut - to both amateurs and professional clock repairmen. For the last fifteen years, he has owned and operated a clock repair store in New York state.

www.ingramcontent.com/pod-product-compliance
Lightning Source LLC
Chambersburg PA
CBHW060649280326
41933CB00012B/2182